CRIMSON REMNANTS

A COLLECTION OF POETRY

SHINEPREET KAUR

Contents

Contents

Preface

the quiet spaces between these words
are language of a soul, moments captured
and a tapestry of raw emotion
I invite you all to pause, breathe
And read....

Acknowledgements

i would like to express my deepest desire to thank all of you who chose to pick up this book even when you had millions other options.

Chapter 1

Crimson remnants
are the whisper of a heart
Which were once whole
Now fractured and forlorn

Chapter2

A fierce heart is grown
When you fight your demons
On your own.

Chapter3

Let the dawn break through the night
With fragile hands, reclaim the shine,
For though the past may cast its hue,
A brighter path awaits for you

Chapter4

Two souls in the cosmos
Love unfathomably

Chapter5

Another year, another day,
The calendar turns but she can't stay,
The eagerness to hide from the world still
Remains and she waits with her hope
In a hideous place.
She feels the joy, the festal cheer,
For birthday's bring very dark near.
The cake a symbol sweet and bright,
Is ponderous in her trembling sight.
Each candle's flicker fleeting small,
Feels like a shadow's silent call.
A cake is cut and wishes are made,
She sees the years ahead of her in
A dark parade.
A march towards the gift she fears,
More than the crowd,
More than the cheers.
In quiet moments, she will sigh,
And let the years go drifting by
For in her heart the truth is stark
Each birthday brings her one step towards
The dark.

Chapter 6

In a sky blue turban
He stands so tall
A ray of love
In a world so small
With a shirt so white
A symbol so pure
A guardian's touch
Forever sure

Chapter 7

In the hush of twilight
a heart is refrain,
crimson tears and remnants of pain.
Fragments scattered,
Love's soft trace.
Hope begins in a broken space.

Chapter8

Just as a raindrop waited to kiss the ground,
Fire searched for wood,
Water awaited for thirst,
And earth longed for moon,
I was hoping to hold you.

Chapter 9

But whispers in the dark grow
Loud and wild,
With chains of reason tightly bound,
The poets, the shadows are exiled,
In a world where their voices are drowned.
For the city fears the truth they promised,
The echoes of a world gone wrong,
So they silence the poet's name,
As the ink runs dry beneath the sky.
Yet in the silence, a ghostly cry,
The poet's words linger forever undying,
A truth that no blade can ever belie,
In their death they are not truly dying.

Chapter 10

In every gentle sway of the flower
I see your laugh as bright as day.
The flower's grace,
So tender true.
Reminds me always of you.

Chapter11

In the cold days of despair
The warmth of books keeps me alive

Chapter 12

They whisper threats but he sits still,
Lost in his mind's intricate maze.
In the quiet of room where shadows creep,
He eyes the night with a weary gaze.
Outside the darkness roams with glide,
But here within
It is just the night.

Chapter 13

The fortitude of today's women is unwavering.
Born from fire's womb
like Draupadi.
and like Rani Padmini
you choose to burn but never plead.

Chapter 14

Dreams said under one's breath now fade to gray,
As love turns anguish,
And hope slips away.
Identity lost in echo of pain,
A life once vibrant,
Now weathered by rain.

Chapter 15

They think I killed myself
But can't you see all the pain
You put me through
All the truths you never told me
Those sweet lies that I once believed
Now I bleed through my veins made of steel.
Yes, I was miserable
But I had grace
Now I am dying
Because the truths are clutching
My throat with a crimson lace.

Chapter16

The beauty of love is
Even when apart.
It is a secret kept gently,
Deep in our heart.

Chapter 17

Mumma
My world my steadfast star
In your arms
I am cherished
No matter how far
Thank you for being my guiding light
In your love
I bloom
Forever in flight

Chapter18

With every soft peek
She feels his embrace
A rhythm of desolation
A celestial grace.
He looks at her
Eyes soft aglow
Like the moon looks at earth
In the dead of night.

Chapter19

The vermillion of an indian bride
Shines bright like fire.
The promise of forever
Through all the storms
Of their life.

Chapter20

then his disdainful eyes
met her adoring eyes
and lilies fell from the sky

Chapter21

In the quiet of night
Where shadows blend
She loved a monster
And met her end.

Chapter22

My eyes are filled with dreams,
A wistful ache
Each glance is longing,
Each breathe a mistake.
She dances in the shadows
With her feelings confined.
Loving from distance
Where hopes intertwine.

Chapter 23

She leaps and strives and gives her all,
Yet every time she seems to fall,
Her dreams are tangled in a fray,
Her efforts lost in a disarray.
She wants to shout, to cry, to whine,
"Look can't you see! I chase the dream!
I'm giving more than I can spare, I'm here,
I'm trying, do you care? "

Chapter 24

they thought the silence
was the display of her weakness.
But little did they know
that beneath the calm
a storm had been made.
She plots her revenge
with a fire within her fierce and unturned.

Chapter25

I am the story yet to be written,
A journey of strength, unbidden
I am the soil beneath my feet,
I am the sunrise breaking free.

Chapter26

and in the end of at it all
i walked away even though it tore me apart.

Chapter 27

A crazy crowd
But she stands alone,
Her heart is screaming
A delicate tone.
Just as an ephemeral dream
He passes by,
Her idol's gaze,
A far-flung light.

Chapter28

In the silence between us,
Your green eyes hide,
A word of soft whispers,
Where secrets reside.
I watch from a distance,
Heart racing, yet still,
Yearning to break through your quiet,
Sweet will.
Each glance is a story,
Untold and sincere,
In your shy, gentle heart,
I long to draw near With patience I wait,
our worlds softly blend,
Hoping one day,
Your silence will end.

Chapter29

Inside my heart there is a secret that grows
it is the love i feel
but never dare expose
my words get tangled
always lost in my mind
the courage slips away with no peace to find.

Chapter30

But for now let me hold my love close to me
for it is unspoken like a deep hurt

Chapter 31

we were once two souls tangled with grace
and look now
suddenly strangers
both lost in this race.

Chapter32

my love lives in the ink
where reality fades.
a devotion unstated
but in my heart it is true.

Chapter 33

your path is my compass
your way is my home
i will walk through the storm with you
for when we are together the journey's just began.

Chapter34

i write his name on the canvas of night
achingly hoping the stars will bring him back to light
but the heavens are mute
and stars don't reply
so i wait for him with tears in my eyes.

Chapter35

in every song there is a spark which rises him high
so everynight he dreams of her in the cool of night
expecting to touch her or meeting face to face
his love is endless even if he falls from grace.

Chapter36

those ghostly calls were all around
like it was the time of stone and timbered walls.
there was Elise , standing in grief
for a love she expected but never received.
they all spoke in voices so stern
for duty's path and vexation to earn.
a suitor grand was chosen for her.
"Must i be sold like a silken thread"
cried Elise with a face so red
hoping her words would waver her guardian's objectionable plans.

Chapter37

he is a star whose presence feels so rare
a name that echoes in the air
i send my thoughts out like a spell
to where my lucky angels dwell.
hoping him to look for the signs
and claim me as his star.

Chapter38

i choose to watch a building burn to ashes
but not you walking away from me.
For you are the only place i can call home.

Chapter39

i see the storm outside of my house.
it reminds me of all the things i am
and all the things i wish i could be
and then i feel the cold breeze on my face
again as a reminder to live in the moment.
To kick the worries out and forget the past .

Chapter40

every night when i tried to sleep
the past creeped up on me
like a web spiralling across
my mind , body and soul.
a part of me wants to let go of this world
and the other wants to hang onto my dear life.
though every breath is a struggle, each step a fright
yet, beneath this pain something stirs
compelling me to hang onto my dear life.